Happy Pets, Healthy Pets

by Alison Auch

Content and Reading Adviser:
Mary Beth Fletcher, Ed.D.
Educational Consultant/Reading Specialist
The Carroll School, Lincoln, Massachusetts

Spyglass
BOOKS

COMPASS POINT BOOKS

Minneapolis, Minnesota

Compass Point Books
3109 West 50th Street, #115
Minneapolis, MN 55410

Visit Compass Point Books on the Internet at *www.compasspointbooks.com*
or e-mail your request to *custserv@compasspointbooks.com*

Photographs ©: Corbis, cover (left); PhotoDisc, cover (right), 1, 5 (left), 18; Comstock, 4 (left), 5 (middle), 19; Jeremy Horner/Corbis, 4 (right); Skjold Photographs, 5 (right); Norvia Behling, 6, 8, 10, 14, 15; Laura Dwight/Corbis, 7, 11; Cheryl A. Ertelt, 9; Kent & Donna Dannen, 12; Fotografia, Inc./Corbis, 13; Paul Barton/Corbis, 16; Joe McDonald/Corbis, 17.

Project Manager: Rebecca Weber McEwen
Editors: Heidi Schoof and Patricia Stockland
Photo Researcher: Svetlana Zhurkina
Designer: Jaime Martens
Illustrator: Anna-Maria Crum

Library of Congress Cataloging-in-Publication Data
Auch, Alison.
  Happy pets, healthy pets / by Alison Auch.
       p. cm. — (Spyglass books)
Summary: Describes common household pets, what makes them enjoyable to
own, and ways to care for them.
Includes bibliographical references (p.   ).
  ISBN 0-7565-0454-6 (hardcover)
  1. Pets—Juvenile literature. [1. Pets.] I. Title. II. Series.
  SF416.2 .A83 2003
  636.088'7—dc21   2002012629

Contents

NOTE: Glossary words are in *bold* the first time they appear.

All Kinds of Pets

Pets come in many shapes and sizes. A pet can be a big dog. A pet can be a small guinea pig.

All pets need people to take care of them.

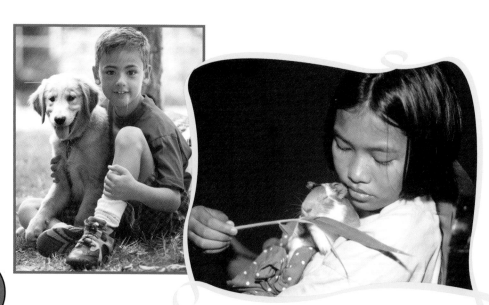

What a Pet!

Did you know some people
have turtles, horses, and
llamas for pets?

Safe at Home

Like you, pets need a warm, safe home to live in.

Tiny Homes

Gerbils, hamsters, and guinea
pigs need to live in cages.
They are too small to run free.

Water, Water Everywhere!

Like you, pets need fresh, clean water to drink.

8

Slurp, Slurp!

Dogs drink their water out
of bowls. Some dogs like
to drink from the toilet
bowl. Yuck!

Good Food

Like you, pets need plenty of good food to eat.

Munch, munch!

Pet rabbits should not eat much lettuce. It can upset their stomachs.

Hot and Cold

Like you, pets need to be **protected** from hot and cold weather.

In the Doghouse

Dogs who spend time outside need a warm, dry *shelter.*

Vets for Pets

Like you, pets need doctors when they are sick.

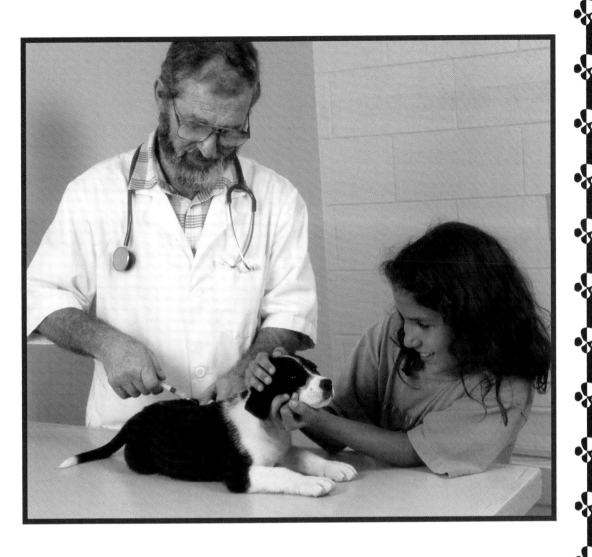

Healthy Pets

Pets need to see a *veterinarian* for checkups and shots to stay healthy.

Walk, Run, and Jump

Like you, pets need exercise to stay healthy.

Pets on the Move

Cats love to chase things such as string tied to a stick, or a buzzing fly!

Lots of Love

Like you, pets need a lot of love.

Love for the Little Guy

It's not easy to kiss a fish or hug a hamster! You can love them by taking good care of them.

Did You Know?

People in *ancient* Egypt loved their cats. When the cats died, the people would shave off their eyebrows to show how sad they were.

Dogs were the first animals that people had as pets. Dogs helped people hunt and kept them safe.

Being around pets can help keep people happy and healthy. Some special pets go to *hospitals* to cheer up sick people.

Some dogs are working dogs. They may help to *herd* cattle or sheep.

21

Glossary

ancient–something from a long time ago

herd–to make animals or people move together as a group

hospital–a place where doctors and nurses take care of people who are sick or hurt

protect–to guard or keep something safe

shelter–a place where you can keep covered in bad weather, or stay safe from danger

veterinarian–a doctor who takes care of animals

Learn More

Books

Morgan, Sally. *Animals as Friends.*
   New York: Franklin Watts, 1999.
Royson, Angela. *Pets.* Crystal Lake, Ill.:
   Heinemann Interactive Library, 1997.
Schaefer, Lola M. *Family Pets.*
   Mankato, Minn.: Pebble Books, 1999.

Web Sites

ASPCA

www.animaland.org/petcare/

Central Pets

www.centralpets.com/
   (click on a pet category for pet care
   information; also try the fun games)

Index

GR: F

Word Count: 98

From Alison Auch

Reading and writing are my favorite things to do. When I'm not reading or writing, I like to go to the mountains or play with my little girl, Chloe.

24